# Celebrate Today!

## DISCOVERING THE WONDER OF LIFE'S LITTLE JOYS

## Kim Jacobs

HARVEST HOUSE PUBLISHERS
EUGENE, OREGON

*A happy life is not built up of tours*

*abroad and pleasant holidays,*

*but of little clumps of violets*

*noticed by the roadside, hidden*

*away almost so that only those can*

*see them who have God's peace*

*and love in their hearts.*

EDWARD WILSON

*I* look upon life as a gift from God.
I did nothing to earn it.

*Joyce Cary*

*I*f the sight of the blue skies fills you with joy,
if a blade of grass springing up in the fields has
power to move you, if the simple things of
nature have a message that you
understand, rejoice, for
your soul is alive . . .

*Eleonora Duse*

*H*e enjoys true
leisure who has time to
improve his soul's estate.

Henry David Thoreau

*I doubt whether the world holds for
anyone a more soul-stirring surprise
than the first adventure with ice cream.*

Heywood C. Broun

*I*t is a wonderful thing to
be alive! If a person lives to
be very old, let him rejoice
in every day of life...

The Book of Ecclesiastes

Kim Jac

*I* believe that this world was set about for us to enjoy and to love and to experience and to have it all be, to a certain extent, unpredictable.

*Judith Jamison*

*S*ome people are making such thorough plans for rainy days that they aren't enjoying today's sunshine.

*William Feather*

There is a need to discover that we are capable of solitary joy and having experienced it, know that we have touched the core of self.

*Barbara Lazear Ascher*

The air is like a butterfly. With frail blue wings. The happy earth looks at the sky. And sings.

*Joyce Kilmer*

Happiness is a sort of atmosphere you can live in sometimes when you're lucky. Joy is a light that fills you with hope and faith and love.

*Adela Rogers St. Johns*

*F*ind ecstasy in life; the mere
sense of living is joy enough.

*Emily Dickinson*

*W*hen you come right down to it,
the secret of having it all is loving it all.

*Joyce Brothers*

*T*he secret of joy in
work is contained in one word,
excellence. To know how to do
something well is to enjoy it.

*Pearl Buck*

*J*oy is what happens to
us when we allow ourselves
to recognize how good
things really are.

*Marianne Williamson*

*I* have come finally to a simple
philosophy of work. I enjoy what I do
and do the best I can. That is enough.

*Maria Schell*

KimJacobs©

*M*y observation [is] that
most men that do thrive in the
world forget to take pleasure during
the time that they are getting their
estate, but reserve that till they have got one,
and then it is too late for them to enjoy it.

*Samuel Pepys*

*T*he reflections
on a day well spent
furnish us with joys
more pleasing than ten
thousand triumphs.

*Thomas à Kempis*

The secret of contentment is knowing how to enjoy what you have, and to be able to lose all desire for things beyond your reach.

*Lin Yu-t'ang*

Set me a task in which I can put something of my very self, and it is a task no longer; it is joy; it is art.

*Bliss Carman*

Cobblestone Lane

Market

Saturday

The key to the mystery of a great
artist is that for reasons unknown,
he will give away his energies and
his life just to make sure that one note
follows another inevitably . . . and
leaves us with the feeling that
something is right in the world.

*Leonard Bernstein*

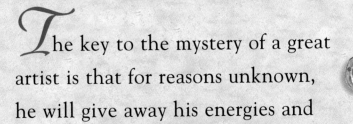

Focus on the journey,
not the destination. Joy
is found not in finishing
an activity but in doing it.

*Greg Anderson*

At books, or work, or healthy play,
Let all my years be passed;
That I may give for every day
A good account at last.

Isaac Watts

*Like what you do, if you don't like it, do something else.*

Paul Harvey

**W**hatever is good and perfect comes to us from God, the Creator of all light, and he shines forever without change or shadow...

*The Book of James*

**T**here may be Peace without Joy, and Joy without Peace, but the two combined make Happiness.

*John Buchan*

**S**ilence is the perfectest herald of joy: I were but little happy if I could say how much.

*William Shakespeare*

*A joy that's shared is
a joy made double.*

English Proverb

*The joyous time is when
the breeze first strikes
your sails, and the waters
rustle under your bows.*

Charles Buxton

Life itself cannot give
you joy, unless you really
will it. Life just gives you
time and space—it's up to
you to fill it.

Chinese Proverb

There are no little events in life,
those we think of no consequence
may be full of fate, and it is at
our own risk if we neglect the

acquaintances and opportunities
that seem to be casually offered,
and of small importance.

*Amelia Barr*

I have inspiration and feelings
of being alive most every day I live.
I call them part of the joy
of living, and they are
there for all of us.

*Judy Collins*

*Y*ou must learn day by day, year by year, to broaden your horizons. The more things you love, the more you are interested in, the more you enjoy...

*Ethel Barrymore*

*L*earning . . .
should be
a joy and full
of excitement.
It is life's greatest
adventure; it is an
illustrated excursion into
the mind of noble and learned men . . .

*Taylor Caldwell*

*I*s it so small a thing
To have enjoy'd the sun,
To have lived light in the spring,
To have loved, to have thought, to have done?

*Matthew Arnold*

*I* cannot believe
that the inscrutable
universe turns on
an axis of
suffering; surely
the strange beauty of the world must
somewhere rest on pure joy!

*Louise A. Bogan*

*T*hings to remember:
1) The worth of character;
2) The improvement of talent;
3) The influence of example;
4) The joy of origination;
5) The dignity of simplicity;
6) The success of perseverance.

*Marshall Field*

*The joy of the mind is the measure of its strength.*
*Ninon de Lenclos*

*I* arise in the morning torn between a desire to improve (or save) the world and a desire to enjoy (or savor) the world. This makes it hard to plan the day.

*E. B. White*

*T*hose who bring sunshine
into the lives of others,
cannot keep it from themselves.

*James Matthew Barrie*

*W*hen dreams
come true at last,
there is life and joy.

*The Book of Proverbs*

*Joy is not in things, it is in us.*

Richard Wagner

Happiness is a rare plant, that seldom takes root on earth—few ever enjoyed it, except for a brief period; the search after it is rarely rewarded by the discovery. But, there is an admirable substitute for it . . . a contented spirit.

*Lady Marguerite Blessington*

If the day and the night are such that you greet them with joy, and life emits a fragrance like flowers and sweet-scented herbs—that is your success . . .

*Henry David Thoreau*

The art of being happy lies
in the power of extracting
happiness from common things.

*Henry Ward Beecher*

The more you praise and
celebrate your life, the more
there is in life to celebrate.

*Author Unknown*

He will yet fill your
mouth with laughter and
your lips with shouts of joy.

*The Book of Job*

*H*ave regular hours for
work and play; make each day
both useful and pleasant, and
prove that you understand the
worth of time by employing it well.
Then youth will be delightful, old age
will bring few regrets, and life will
become a beautiful success.

*Louisa May Alcott*

*I*f you do a good job for others,
you heal yourself at the same time,
because a dose of joy is a spiritual cure.
It transcends
all barriers.

*Ed Sullivan*

$\mathcal{L}$et's go and see everybody," said Pooh. "Because when you've been walking in the wind for miles, and you suddenly go into somebody's house, and he says, 'Hallo, Pooh, you're just in time for a little smackerel of something,' and you are, then it's what I call a Friendly Day."

*A. A. Milne*

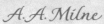

*$\mathcal{A}$ wise man sings his joys in the closet of his heart.*

*Tibullus*

You're a happy fellow,
for you'll give happiness
and joy to many other people.
There is nothing better
or greater than that!

*Ludwig van Beethoven*

Work joyfully and peacefully,
knowing that right thoughts and
right efforts will inevitably bring
about right results.

*James Allen*

The best
way to pay
for a lovely
moment is
to enjoy it.

*Richard Bach*

*A*h, what a grand,
glorious day this has been.

*Charlotte Forten Grimke*